SAVE THE U.S. ECONOMY
FROM COLLAPSE

Eliminate the National Debt in 10 years

Chapters

1. Introduction

With the $14.3 trillion dollar national debt the U.S. has the potential of economic collapse. A collapse of this magnitude would make the Great Depression of the 1930s look like child's play. The unemployment rate would go to 25%, the price of oil would go to $300 a barrel and the price of food would soar. If the U.S. economy should collapse because of the national debt there could be riots in the streets of our cities because nearly 50% of the population is on some form of welfare. Social Security, government pension and Medicare checks could stop.

There would be a domino effect and economies around the world would collapse. The dollar would be weaker than the Indian Rupee or Mexican Peso. It would cause both financial and social instability around the world. The collapse of the U.S. economy could trigger a world war. The politicians in Washington are trying to sweep the magnitude of this problem under the rug by telling us not to worry about it. Don't believe them. This is a very serious problem more so than the terrorist attacks on September 11th 2001, more so than the Great Depression.

What makes the U.S. the dominant world power is our economy. What keeps the world stable is the U.S. economy and allows us to have the world's most powerful military force. Even if the economy doesn't collapse and the U.S. should become a second rate economy it would have a major impact on world stability. It may even trigger a world war.

The biggest threat to the existence of the United States is not a foreign military power but our national debt. Our very existence centers on the Constitution and our economic power. If we should fail as the number one economic power we may fail as a nation. Osama Bin Laden, the master mind of the September 11th 2001 knew that to conquer the U.S. you must first bring down its economy. If our economy fails then everything below it fails including our military. Once our economy fails then we cease to exist as a military power. From there a foreign power can easily conquer us. The current national debt has the potential of collapsing the U.S. economy.

This book describes a realistic plan to eliminate the national debt and save the U.S. economy.
The U.S. national debt as of this writing is $14.3 trillion dollars. The U.S. national debt is about 100% of the Gross Domestic Product (GDP). For a nation, company or even an individual that is a terrible situation to be in. On a personal level you would be terrified if your credit card debt balances equaled your gross income. We should all be terrified the national debt is equal to the GDP. Every time there is a budget deficit it gets added to the national debt.
This book describes an easy way to eliminate the national debt in 10 years without raising taxes, reducing Social Security benefits, raising the Social Security retirement age, reducing Medicare, cutting defense spending or drastically cutting social programs. Here are the typical ways our politicians want to solve the problem. All of them are stupid and won't work.

I've read and heard a lot of ideas from politicians and pundits of how to reduce the national debt. Nobody in Washington is thinking "outside of the box" on this issue. All ideas just reduce the national debt. It's like everyone in Washington has tunnel vision. The plan described in this book definitely thinks "outside the box" and **ELIMINATES** the national debt. Politicians and their tunnel vision can only think of draconian cuts in spending or massive tax hikes. It's as if there is no imagination on the part of Washington politicians.

This book describes a plan that dramatically grows the economy which in turn dramatically increases federal government tax revenues without drastic cuts in entitlement programs and defense spending. The plan is a multi-point plan which I describe in detail and it definitely is "outside the box" thinking. If this multi-point plan were to become law in the U.S. world confidence in our economy would be restored. Restoring confidence in the U.S. economy would have a stabilizing affect on other world economies.

2. Politicians say "Cut Spending"

For FY2012 there have been various calls to slash federal spending. That looks great on paper but in reality someone or something loses funding and they don't like it. Special interest groups, unions or federal employees are negatively affected and then the fight begins usually resulting in protests, sometime riots and always in stalemate. One party or interest group accuses the other party of trying to reduce or eliminate Medicare. Radically cutting spending will cause a lot of problems especially if it's an entitlement program. If a person is receiving benefits from an entitlement program and the benefits suddenly stops it's unfair and that person becomes angry. The proper way to cut spending is gradually over time.

3. Politicians say "Raise Taxes"

To reduce the deficit politicians in one party are always advocating tax increases or at minimum raising taxes on who they perceive as the wealthy. The same politicians want to punish those greedy corporations. What they don't realize is the so-called greedy corporations are the ones who hire people and create jobs. If you tax the so-called greedy corporations they will have less money to hire people. In FY2011 the federal budget deficit was $1.3 trillion dollars. What the "raise taxes" politicians don't realize is if you taxed everyone making over $250K 100% of all their money that would only cover 1/3rd of the deficit. Raising taxes would also reduce economic activity and do just the opposite of generating additional revenue for the government.

4. The Debt Ceiling Limit

Let's understand what the debt ceiling is all about. Some people call the debt ceiling the nation's credit card. I wish it worked more like a credit card where you had a credit limit and a credit balance. With a credit card if the balance is equal to the credit limit you have no more available credit. However, if you pay a chunk to the credit card balance the difference is the new credit available to you. Whoever structured the national debt and debt ceiling wasn't thinking clearly.

As of this writing FY2011 there is talk of raising the debt ceiling limit. Some say we must do it and others say don't do it. When the national debt reaches the debt ceiling limit, by law the Department of the Treasury cannot borrow any more money. Personally I would not increase the credit limit of a compulsive spender. The U.S. is a compulsive spender. In theory I'm against raising the debt ceiling but in reality I know we must raise the debt ceiling limit because of the way our debt is structured.

On the revenue income side taxes trickle in asynchronously from small businesses, corporations, individuals and payroll withholdings by corporations. On the expenditure side expense outlays such as Social Security checks, military pensions are more constant. Each month like clockwork checks go out. If a private company had this problem they would set up a revolving line of credit with a bank. For expenses money would be pulled down from the bank and when receipts came in the company would pay back to the bank that amount owed preserving the line of credit.

The federal government doesn't do that. Because expenses are greater than the tax revenues we borrow 40 cents for each expense dollar. Even when tax revenues come in the debt is never paid back because the expenses are so much greater than the revenue. Expenses such as Social Security checks are possibly borrowed which adds to the national debt. Revenues are never returned to lower the debt. If the debt limit ceiling isn't raised people may not get their Social Security checks. Doctors may not receive Medicare payments. Sorry, we have no choice but to raise the debt ceiling until we can get tax revenues to be greater than expenses. Getting tax revenues greater than federal expenses is the key to the success of this plan. Keep reading and you'll understand how we can make this happen.

5. So what is the Easy Way to Eliminate the National Debt?

As I previously mentioned we can't just slash spending or raise taxes over night. That will have negative effects on our society and economy. Some will think we can do both. That's a double negative for the U.S. economy. It took a long time for the U.S. to get to this terrible economic state and it will take time to correct it. The way to get out of this terrible economic state is what I call "Freeze and Grow". Freeze the federal budget at the FY2008 level for 10 years and dramatically grow the economy. Grow the U.S. GDP from $14.3 to $22 trillion dollars by 2021. Some will say that's impossible but it's very achievable with this plan.

I have firsthand experience with this philosophy of "Freeze and Grow". On a personal level in 2007 I had quite a bit of debt mainly due to paying off my daughter's student loans. My total debt minus my mortgage was nearly 90% of my gross pay. Then something astonishing happened. I lost my job. My severance package amounted to 6 months of salary continuation. I found a job very quickly for the same salary. For 6 months my salary doubled and I used the extra money to pay off my debts. I was much disciplined and resisted the temptation to use my extra windfall of income to purchase something. Each payday I applied the extra income to my debt. In 6 months with the exception of my mortgage I was debt free. If it can work for me on a personal level it can work for the federal government on a grand level. Using the philosophy "a rising tide raises all boats" this plan will get most states out of debt at the same time.

Here is the plan to eliminate the national debt in 10 years. This is a multi-point plan requiring all points of the plan be implemented simultaneously.

1. Freeze the federal budget for 10 years at FY2008 level.
2. Change the tax code to motivate hyper economic activity.
3. Change Social Security contributions by eliminating the caps.
4. Become totally energy independent.
5. Stop the flow of illegal aliens into the country.
6. Reduce all useless regulations on small and large businesses.
7. Remove all useless environmental regulations that impair or hamper companies.

Have you ever seen the U.S. national debt counter? If not click on http://www.usdebtclock.org/. It's continuously counting up. The first goal is to get the debt counter to stop. Stopping means the U.S. has achieved a balance budget and is not adding the budget deficit to the national debt. The second goal is to get the counter to decrement. The final goal is to get the counter to count down to zero.

6. The National Debt

$14,353,269,414,309.87

This proposal does require congress to be disciplined. The goal is to do everything possible to let the business community thrive and grow thus hire more people. It requires congress to keep within the FY2008 spending limits for 10 years. It also requires congress to apply all revenue surpluses to the principal of the national debt. Using this plan there will be no need to increase the retirement age for anyone on Social Security, no means testing, no reduction in Social Security benefits. With the exception of weeding out waste, fraud and abuse there would be no need to reduce Medicare benefits to anyone. No need to reduce defense spending. There would be no need to reduce social programs such as Head Start or Pell Grants. When this philosophy was actually applied to my personal experience as I describe earlier, I didn't reduce my lifestyle or standard of living at all. However, I didn't increase my lifestyle or standard of living either which is essential to maintaining the discipline to use the extra revenue to pay off the debt.

Here is each section of this proposal in more detail.

7. Freeze the federal budget at FY2008 level

In order for the plan to work the federal budget has to be frozen at the FY2008 level for 10 years. It makes no sense to drastically grow the economy and still increase spending. While the budget is frozen there is no need to raise the Social Security retirement age. No reason to reduce benefits. No reason to reduce Medicare medical coverage or slash social programs. The FY2008 budget was quite generous with entitlement programs. No reason to reduce defense or Homeland Security funding. It would make sense to wind down the Iraq and Afghanistan war funding and apply it to other needed programs but not increasing overall FY2008 budget funding.

8. Change the tax system

In order to make this plan work the current tax system has to be scrapped and changed to allow economic growth. This plan proposes a bold replacement of the current income tax system.

The current tax system in America is what is holding our economy back. The current tax system is and always has been a burden on the economy. The politicians believe more revenue comes into the government if taxes are raised. The opposite is true. There is an assumption in Washington and state capitals that the economy is static and always has the same size and activity. In fact the economy is dynamic in nature. The expansion of the economy is actually opposite to taxes and the tax rate. If taxes go up the growth, expansion and velocity of the economy goes down. If taxes go down the growth, expansion and velocity of the economy goes up. There is history to back this up.

In October of 1929 when the stock market crashed there was no depression. The crash just started a down turn in the economy. President Herbert Hoover and congress decided to raise taxes and increase spending to stimulate the economy. His administration and congressional actions made things a lot worse. Those actions caused the Great Depression which lasted for nearly 12 years. The result was there was less money in the hands of people, small business and corporations. There was less money in circulation causing the economy to slow down. President Roosevelt made the problem worse by increasing federal spending and the beginning of budget deficits. By the start of World War II the unemployment rate was still 17%.

In 1962 the economy was entering into a bad recession. President Kennedy did the opposite of FDR and asked the congress to lower taxes across the board to stimulate the economy. Even though he died before he could see it, the economy was booming in the mid '60s even with the Vietnam War. In 1981 the country entered into another deep recession. President Reagan asked congress to lower taxes. It worked so well by 1988 over 22 million jobs were created. The saying "if you want to stop something then tax it" is very true. The opposite also holds true. If you want to stimulate the economy reduce taxes and put more money into people's hands. This plan would put a lot more money in people's hands and increase the velocity of money thus causing the economy to speed up dramatically.

The current federal income tax system in the United States is a complicated mess. The tax code is hard to understand, much too complicated and very unfair. Nearly 50% of Americans pay no income tax. The other 50% are **paying** for those who don't pay anything at all. This plan suggests a true FLAT but low income tax system applied to all Americans.

"The democracy will cease to exist when you take away from those who are willing to work and give to those who would not." – Thomas Jefferson

Proposal:

Change the tax system so all people, corporations and capital in America would pay a flat tax on income of 5%. With such a tax system there would be no deductions, no exemptions, no loop holes, nothing. Nobody is excluded. Nothing is deductible or exempt on earned wages. Everyone in America would pay income tax at the same low rate. Whatever your income is you would pay 5% income tax on it. Interest earnings would be taxed at 5%. Corporate profits would be taxed at 5%. Capital would be taxed at 5%

Recent data from the U.S. Department of the Treasury shows for fiscal year FY2010 Income tax revenues were $899 billion dollars, Social Security revenues were $865 billion dollars and other revenues such as corporate and excise taxes were $399 billion dollars for total revenues of $2.2 trillion dollars. Past history has shown that lowering taxes actually increases revenue to both state and federal governments. It also increases economic activity which increases hiring in the private sector. Small business and large corporations taxed less mean increased hiring activity.

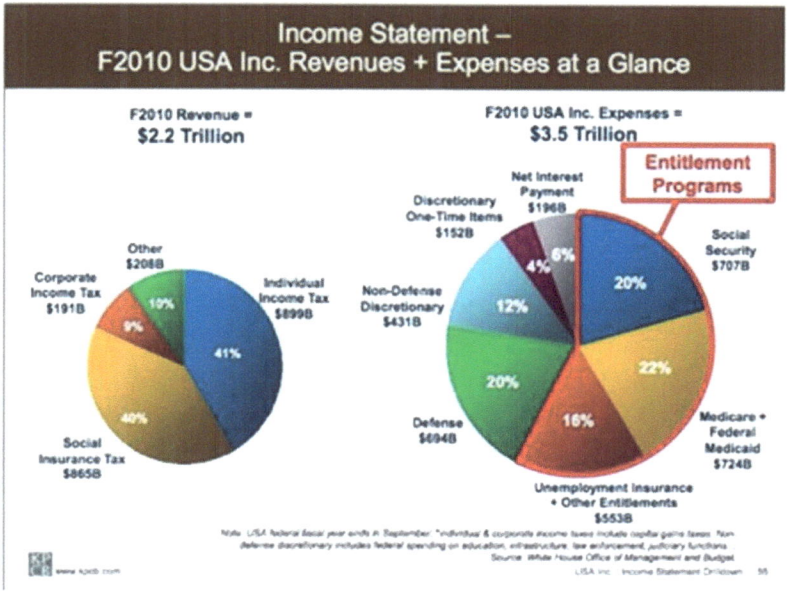

As people have more money to spend they will purchase and consume more products and services. Small businesses and large corporations will have a harder time keeping up with increased demand forcing them to hire more people. Every time money changes hands it's taxed by the government. If there is more money in people's hands there is more consumption and increased economic activity. The government revenues would increase which would lower the budget deficit to zero and even provide a surplus. **Apply all income tax surpluses to the national debt for 10 years.**

Questions and Answers:

Q: Would all Americans have to pay income tax?
A: Yes, it's the only fair thing to do. All Americans would have a stake in our economy and government. No more 50% of the people paying for the other 50%. A 5% tax rate is so low everyone can afford it.

Q: Would higher income earners pay more income tax?
A: Yes. The more money you earn the more you would pay but everyone would pay 5% of their income. Example; if a person earned $100 they would pay $5.00 in taxes. If a person earned $1000 they would pay $50.00 in income taxes. It's that simple and that low.

Q: If everyone pays 5% wouldn't government revenues go down?
A: On the contrary, government revenues would increase. Being taxed at 5% would put more money into people's pocket. Generally most people in America are consumers. The more money they have the more they spend and consume. This is good for both business and government. Businesses will hire more people with increased business activity. The more people hired the more tax revenues the federal and state governments get.

Q: Are there any negative affects to this plan?
A: Yes. The role of the IRS would be greatly reduced. With a flat tax there would be no need for many people to file taxes. No deductions to worry about. The employers would withhold 5% of whatever a person's income is and send it into the federal government.

Q: Would Americans adapt to this plan?
A: Yes, easily. Americans already pay a flat FICA tax of 7.5% and a flat Medicare tax of 1.25% of their income.

Q: Could this help reduce the national debt?
A: Yes! Revenues would increase dramatically. Congress would have to be disciplined and take any surplus revenue and apply it to the national debt.

Q: Can you guarantee revenues would dramatically increase?
A: Can't guarantee anything but look at the FY2010 revenues. Social Security at 7.5% with income caps is a flat tax and almost equals the total revenues of all the income taxes. With the current tax system only 50% of the people are paying income tax. If all the people, 100% of wage earners were paying a 5% flat tax, income tax receipts would probably double. By the way, if the caps were removed from Social Security those revenue receipts would also likely double. The U.S. Government would be awash in revenue while the people would be taxed less and have more money in their pockets.

9. Change Social Security contributions by eliminating the caps

In order to make this plan work Social Security needs a minor 'tweak' which would double revenues into the fund. All surplus revenues over the amount needed to fund Social Security would be used to pay down the national debt.

In August of 1935 the congress passed the Social Security Act (SSA). The SSA created a social insurance program covering a variety of individuals. The law provided a monthly benefit to individuals' age 65 and older and no longer working. The monthly benefit was paid to the primary worker when he retired; the amount received was based on the individual's payroll tax contributions.

The first recognition of the fragility of the Social Security program occurred in 1975. A report developed by the Treasury Department indicated that Social Security payroll taxes collected would be insufficient to meet Social Security payments by 1979. In response, Congress increased the tax rate, reduced benefits, and made the automatic adjustment to the amount of earnings subject to Social Security independent of the COLA. These steps averted a potential Social Security failure.

In 1983, another potential Social Security crisis was avoided. President Ronald Reagan formed the Greenspan Commission to study the financial state of Social Security. The commission issued a detailed report calling for numerous, sweeping changes to be implemented in order to strengthen Social Security. A bill passed by Congress based upon the recommendations of the Greenspan Commission taxed some Social Security benefits, included federal employees in the definition of employees for Social Security payroll tax purposes, and scheduled increases in the retirement age in the next century.

The fragility of the Social Security system has once again occurred. In 2005 President George W. Bush recommended ways to keep the system from bankruptcy in the near future. In 2005 the Social Security Trust Fund painted a grim picture. Contributions would peak by 2008 and starting in 2018 government payments will exceed contributions. Another dire prediction said the system would be broke or bankrupt by 2037.

The dire situation has accelerated. Currently Social Security is paying out more than it's taking in. The previous estimate predicted Social Security would not be able to meet its obligations was 2018. Contributions into the fund wouldn't meet what it's paying out. The previous estimate is now obsolete due to the recession of 2008. Many older Americans have opted for early retirement putting an enormous strain on the Social Security system. When Social Security was implemented, there were 16 workers for every Social Security recipient; today there are 3.3 workers for every recipient, and it is estimated that by 2030 there will be only two workers for every recipient.

Proposal:
There is one very simple but quick way to keep the fund solvent and even provide fund surpluses. **Remove the income caps on the employee side**. Employers pay 7.5% of an employee's salary to the fund in the form of FICA contributions. The employee also contributes from his or her paycheck 7.5% of their gross wages. Contributions to the trust fund are capped each year. Contributions to the fund stop after the employee has reached a certain gross income or contributed a certain amount for that year. In 2010 FICA contributions were capped at an approximate salary of $108K or $6700 FICA contribution. After that there is no more FICA contributions withheld from an employee's paycheck. By removing the caps there wouldn't be a percentage rate increase in FICA withholdings but much more contributions would go into the fund.

If a person makes less than the salary cap they have FICA withholdings all year from their paycheck. On the other hand, a person such as an athlete or entertainer making equivalent to the salary cap each month would only have to pay the total FICA contribution once ($6700) then they're done. The other eleven months of the year FICA contributions wouldn't be withheld. By removing the salary caps the athlete or entertainer would pay 7.5% of salary or earnings all year. I believe this is fair and the system would benefit with much more needed revenue.

Recent data from the U.S. Department of the Treasury shows for FY 2010 Income tax revenues were $899 billion dollars, Social Security revenues were $865 billion dollars and other revenues such as corporate and excise taxes were $399 billion dollars for total revenues of $2.2 trillion dollars. With the caps in place the Social Security Trust fund received $865 billion dollars. Contributions to the fund would likely double if the caps were removed and all wage and income earners contributed to the fund year round. **Apply all Social Security surpluses to pay down the national debt for 10 years.**

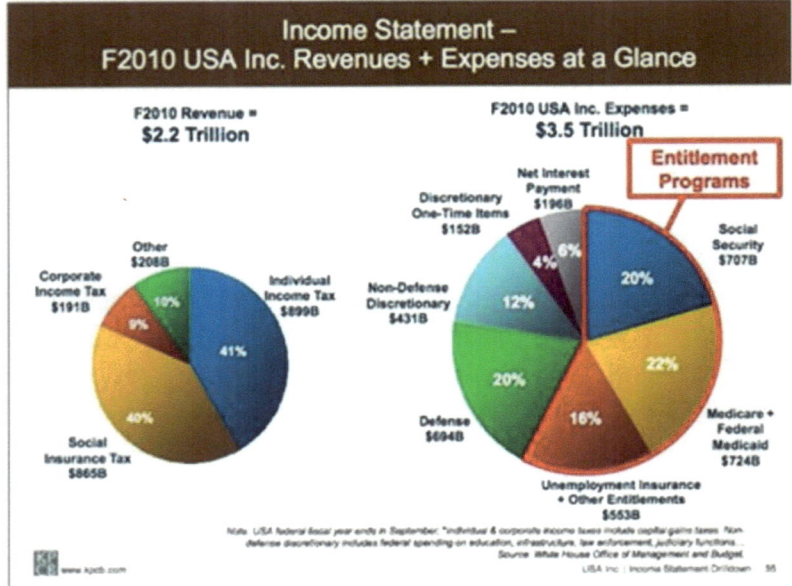

Income Statement –
F2010 USA Inc. Revenues + Expenses at a Glance

Questions and Answers:

Q: Is this fair?
A: Yes. FICA looks and feels like a flat tax. It is a flat tax to those who make under the salary cap. This proposal doesn't increase the percentage withheld but keeps all wage earners contributing throughout the year.

Q: Will some object to this proposal?
A: Yes. Higher than the salary cap wage earners will. The salary caps never made sense. It should be a flat tax imposed equally on all wage earners all year. There are no caps on Medicare contributions so why Social Security contributions.

Q: Will the Social Security system benefit?
A: Yes. Revenues will increase dramatically. In fact there may be such increase in revenues the FICA withholding rate could possibly be reduced.

Q: Who should be contributing to Social Security?
A: Everyone. All persons in America should contribute to the system. No person should be excluded, not congress, not the president, not unions, no one, no exceptions. Some will say they already have a pension plan and shouldn't have to contribute to Social Security. Many people have 401K and IRA retirement plans and still contribute. Everyone should contribute.

Q: Will taking the salary caps off make a difference?
A: Yes it will. Look at FY 2010 revenues. Social Security with the caps almost equaled the individual income tax receipts. Removing the caps will almost double the current Social Security revenues.

Q: Would the retirement age have to be increased or benefits reduced?
A: No to both questions. By removing the caps a flood of increased receipts will come into the Social Security fund. The retirement age could remain the same and the benefits the same.

10.   Become totally energy independent

Cheap Energy! That's a key ingredient to this plan. Keep the cost of a gallon of gasoline below $1.00 a gallon. It's good for the economy and a must for this plan to work.

Currently the U.S. imports 85% of its oil and natural gas from foreign countries. Some of the countries we import oil from are our adversaries. They don't like the U.S. and use oil as an economic and political weapon against us. This dependence on foreign oil leaves our country vulnerable and at great risk. In the past these adversarial countries have embargoed oil exports to the U.S. by cutting off our supply and raising prices. Oil embargoes happened in 1973 and 1979. The oil exporting countries are in a cartel called OPEC. They set prices and production levels which has a destabilizing effect on our economy.

There was a time in the 1980s when geologist thought there was very little oil and natural gas in the U.S. Recent discoveries of huge deposits of offshore oil, shale oil and natural gas have changed that thinking. It is estimated U.S. reserves of oil exceed Saudi Arabia in the form of shale and sand oil. It is also estimated the U.S. has the world's largest reserve of natural gas. For the past 30 years it has been the policy of the U.S. not to drill for additional oil and gas. The environmentalist lobby has done an effective job of putting pressure on congress to stifle U.S. oil and gas exploration and drilling. While we're limiting our oil and gas exploration and drilling efforts the Chinese and Russians are expanding theirs all over the world. This puts the U.S. in a very vulnerable position in the world and potentially threatening our national security.

Currently the federal government has this wild idea that the nation can run itself on alternative energy such as wind, solar and ethanol. Alternative energy can supplement oil and natural gas but not replace it.

In 2008 the price of oil spiked to $150 for a barrel of oil. Gasoline prices spiked to $4.67 a gallon in many states. Because the U.S. isn't energy independent we're subject to political instability and blackmail from other countries. Instability in oil producing countries contributes to the world price of oil. When the price of crude oil increases it's like a cruel tax imposed on the average family. If your car has a 15 gallon gasoline tank and you fill up once a week at $2.50 per gallon your annual cost is $1950 a year. If the price of gasoline goes up to $4.00 per gallon the annual cost nearly doubles to $3120 per year. That's $1170 dollars you don't have to buy other things like clothing, food, shoes for the kids, doctor visits, etc. Because petroleum is used in a variety of products such as plastics everything else is increasing in cost. The cost of shipping, air and train travel also increases. The cost of oil is directly correlated to the inflation rate. If oil prices increase so does the inflation rate. If oil prices decrease so does the inflation rate. The cost of oil directly correlates to consumer spending. If the price of gasoline goes up consumer spending goes down and the reverse is true.

For the past 30 years environmentalists have successfully lobbied congress to halt the building of nuclear power plants and oil refineries. The population in the U.S. has increased to 308 million people per the 2010 census. There have not been any new refineries built in the U.S. since the late 1970s. There has not been any nuclear power plants started since the late 1970s.

The U.S. has the largest deposits of coal in the world. We have developed clean coal technology to power electrical plants. With one of the largest reserves of oil, reserves of natural gas and largest reserves of coal one might think the U.S. should have the lowest energy cost in the world and not be subject political unrest in the world. **Our political leaders have put this nation in a very dangerous predicament.**

It is stupid for the U.S. to be dependent on foreign oil and natural gas.

Proposal:

We should use our vast oil and natural gas resources to power our economy. We should drill internally and offshore immediately so we are not at the mercy of adversarial governments such as Venezuela, Saudi Arabia, Russia and others. It makes no sense to buy oil from them when we have our own. Recent findings show our oil reserves are greater than the entire Middle East. Our reserves of natural gas are the largest in the world.

The U.S. invented nuclear electric power plants. Nuclear power is clean and efficient. One would think as the inventor of this technology we would have many nuclear power plants. On the contrary we have the least of any industrialized country. Nuclear power provides France with 70% of its electricity. In the U.S. only 20% of our electricity is produced by nuclear power plants. We need many more nuclear power plants to provide low cost, clean electricity to fuel our economy. Low cost natural gas and oil will dramatically increase economic activity.

Questions and Answers:

Q: What's the risk if we don't drill and explore for our own oil and gas?
A1: It will hurt our economy. We put the U.S. at risk of not remaining the number one economy in the world. We can also have foreign policy and military risks. We could be bullied by other nations, not being able to field an army, air force and sail a fleet.

A2: It's one of the major causes of inflation. Inflation is directly tied to oil prices. Oil and oil by products are used in our everyday lives. The U.S. being dependent on foreign oil increases inflation. Importing oil has the potential of causing food shortages, food price increases and crashing our economy.

A3: We will not be able to pay off the national debt in 10 years if we continue to have expensive natural gas and oil to run our economy.

Q: Doesn't Ethanol lower the cost of fuel for automobiles?
A: It costs more to produce Ethanol for cars. Ethanol production has a negative effect on our food supply. In the U.S. Ethanol is usually produced from corn. Corn is a major food staple in this country and the rest of the world. Producing Ethanol for cars has actually caused corn supply shortages for food and increased costs. Oil is more efficient than Ethanol in cars as far as miles per gallon (MPG) and cost less overall to produce. Do away with Ethanol from corn.

11. Stop the flow of illegal aliens into the country

A nation's sovereignty is determined how well it protects its borders. A nation has a right to determine who comes in, when and how many. The U.S. has tough immigration laws but the federal government is unwilling to enforce those laws. As a result millions of illegal aliens have come into the U.S. The U.S. welcomes immigrants as long as they follow our immigration laws. The U.S. has the right to meter the flow and monitor who comes into the country. Our borders are broken, especially our southern border. Millions of illegal Mexicans and Latin American people have crossed our boarders without permission. Most illegal immigrants are uneducated and many are illiterate in their own language. As a result when they get to the U.S. which has a much higher cost of living they can only get low paying jobs and need public assistance. **Most receive public assistance in the form of welfare, health care, food stamps and free education.** Some states give illegal aliens driver licenses. In many cases they form gangs and cause crime. 25% of all the inmates incarcerated in California are illegal aliens. This is putting an enormous strain and **cost** on all levels of government. Illegal immigration is literally turning many states into welfare states. Many states such California is on the verge of bankruptcy or financial collapse because of this problem.

Proposal:
Most illegal aliens are seeking jobs. Crack down on employers who hire illegal aliens. Any employer having hired an illegal alien should be fined $10,000 for each person. Deny public assistance such as welfare, food stamps, health care and education. An illegal alien requiring emergency medical treatment should not be denied because the U.S. is a humane country.

Bill the country of origin the medical expenses for their citizen. If the Illegal alien is a Mexican national then invoice Mexico the cost of medical treatment. Why shouldn't Mexico pay for their citizens? After all Mexico is encouraging their citizens to cross into this country illegally. Most illegal aliens from Mexico and Latin America come here for free services. Deny the free services to them.

Create a system where employers can validate the legality of the person applying for a job.

Create a picture Social Security card, showing the picture of the owner. Using E-Verify swipe the card into the system and a picture of the owner from the database appears. If the picture on the display matches the picture on the card the person is legal and can be hired. **Stopping the flow of illegal aliens will dramatically reduce entitlement costs and crime which is essential to this plan.**

Questions and Answers:

Q: How does an employer verify if an employee is in the country legally?
A: Most employers honestly try to verify if an employee is legal. Most use the E-Verify system. Many illegal aliens have forged documents such as Social Security card and driver's license. For about $150 in any big city you can buy forged documents. The Social Security card needs to be updated. In this day and age why does the U.S. still issue paper Social Security cards? The Social Security card should be a laminated card like most driver licenses, have picture ID, thumb print and encoded magnetic strip with your ID information. Proper water marks to make forgery very difficult. An employer should ask for the employee's Social Security card, swipe it through a card reader and E-Verify should display a picture of the person. If the picture matches the employer can hire the person, if not the person should be rejected.

Q: Is it cruel to deny illegal aliens public assistance?
A: No. It's cruel to the U.S. to have millions of citizens from another country on our public assistance such as welfare, Medicaid, Medicare and Social Security. It's cruel when citizens of another country come to this country and commit violent crimes against U.S. citizens. Many U.S. citizens would be alive today if the U.S. prevented illegal aliens from coming into this country. It's cruel the financial strain being put on our government and economy.

Q: Can the U.S. afford to support illegal aliens, citizens from another country?
A: Illegal immigration has the potential of destroying the

country by collapsing our economy.

Q: How about a fraud proof Social Security Card?
A: Why does the U.S. still use a paper Social Security Card? Make a laminated, fraud proof card with a picture ID on it similar to state's driver's license. Employers can swipe the card on a reader connected on line with E-Verify. A picture of the person will come up on the computer screen for comparison. If there is no match the card and the person are fraudulent.

Q: What about crime at the border spilling into the U.S.?
A: Send U.S. armed combat troops to the border as a deterrent to crime on the Mexican side of the border spilling into the U.S. Any excursions into the U.S. should be met with force. In 1916 President Wilson sent the army to guard the southern U.S. border against bandit cross border raids.

12.   Reduce all useless regulations on small and large businesses

Initially regulations on businesses were used to insure safety and health in the workplace and prevent crime and corruption. Initially regulations were never intended to hamper, impair or stifle business operations.

Recently regulations have been used to promote political agendas or ideology of a certain political party or business sector. Additionally, regulations have been used for social engineering or social economic fairness. As an example, the U.S. Fish and Wildlife Service are considering closing the Permian Basin because of what they perceive as an endangered species, the Sand Dune lizard. The Permian basin is privately owned land in Texas and New Mexico and supplies a large percentage of our nation's domestic oil. The net result of over regulation is it handcuffs both small and large businesses causing reduced business opportunities, reduced profits and hiring. Many larger companies are so hampered by regulations from various federal agencies and departments they elect to close and go overseas to foreign countries. This causes job losses and reduced revenue to the federal government. **For this plan to work businesses and jobs have to come back to the U.S.** The more people working in the private sector the more revenue created for the federal government.

Q: Will removing regulations cause safety issues in the workplace?

A: Keep the regulations that insure workplace safety. Keep the regulations that insure no corruption. Remove regulations that have nothing to do with safety, crime and corruption.

13. Remove all useless environmental regulations that impair or hamper companies

When the Environmental Protection Act was created in 1970 I was all for it. It was almost impossible to breathe standing behind a brand new 1969 automobile. The fumes and gasses were terrible if you were stuck in bumper to bumper traffic. I remember you couldn't see the mountains looking down Colorado Blvd. in Pasadena during the summer because of the smog. The rivers of Pittsburgh PA were so polluted they would not freeze in the winter time. The EPA was a wonderful idea but recently it has been used to promote political ideologies, agendas and please special interest groups through regulations.

Since 1970 99% of the pollutants emitted from an automobile have been eliminated. The rivers of Pittsburgh PA and other cities have been cleaned up. Using the EPA regulations to satisfy political agendas and special interest groups hampers business economic activities. Regulations are needed for safety and health but not for political agendas. Businesses have to be free to create opportunities, growth and more jobs. For this plan to work many EPA regulations have to be eliminated to take the handcuffs of businesses so they can expand and create jobs. Businesses creating more jobs results in more tax revenue into the U.S. government.

Q: Will removing regulations cause health problems in the workplace and environment?
A: Keep regulations that make for a healthier workplace and environment. Remove all other regulations that have nothing to do with health and safety.

14.   Conclusion

Using this 7 point plan would eliminate the national debt in 10 years without any reductions in entitlement programs or defense of the nation. As you can see the general idea is to freeze spending at a certain level for 10 years and do everything possible to dramatically grow the economy. The goal is to increase the GDP by 30% in 10 years while freezing the federal budget. The goal is apply all surplus revenue from income tax and Social Security to the national debt for 10 years. By adopting this plan in 2012 the national debt would be gone by 2022.

It does require congress and the president to be disciplined. It does require the U.S. public to be patient. In the long run it will greatly benefit our country for our children and grand children.

By doing nothing and playing politics as usual there will be a financial disaster for our country. Time is up and the national debt clock is counting up to disaster!